BROKEN

SILENCE

The Redeeming Love of God

Kuteshia M. Jackson

Save Me From Myself

You can start to heal when you recognize you have an illness, instead of blowing it off as just my nerves are bad, or it's something "we" just don't get help for."

Below Zero

I go from being depressed

To thirsting with lust and desire

Some days I wake up wondering

Why am I still alive?

When I'm manic, I'm invincible

I have no fear of falling

I hear voices whispering in my ear

Death always calling

Even had the nerve

To take me by the hand

And show me how to fly

Thoughts move faster than the speed of light

I'm always lonely, yet more creative than the average man

I'm told you're ingenious

It won't take long before like a car I break down

Then I'll be locked up again maybe state bound

There is nothing like the feeling of falling

Now I'm alive but feeling nothing at all

Nothing can help me when I'm on a downward spiral

I feel so cold I can't take anymore

On the inside, nothings left

Please save me from myself, please rescue me

I am numb iced up below

Reflection: If you stopped trying to receive happiness through others you would have an excellent life.

Scripture: "We plan the way we want to live, but only God makes us able to live it.
Proverbs 16:9 The Message

Your Thoughts

_____

_____

_____

_____

_____

Need Love

Can you enlighten me

For once can you be straightforward and tell me

Everything that you feel that you think

I just want to know the truth

Even if it hurts me

Tell me now, just be honest

I just want to understand

What's wrong with me

Why do people call me crazy

What can I do to be normal

Tell me

I'll do anything

I'll be anything

I want someone just to love me

I'm begging, PLEASE

Can someone tell

Everything that's wrong with me

Is it because I see things that aren't there

Or hear voices and I stare

Please tell me the truth I don't care

I just want to be loved

Reflection: If you are loyal to God, you do not have to look for love. It is already looking for you!

Scripture: "We know it so well, we're embraced it heart and soul, this love that comes from God.
1 John 4:16 The Message

Your Thoughts

_____

_____

_____

_____

_____

Emotional Rollercoaster

I struggle sometimes

To recognize who I am

As I go from manic to depressed

At time I feel I have a purpose in life

I am so short-sighted

When it comes to my perception of things

Sometimes I think I can see the future

And I that I have wings to fly

There must be a reason I' m crazy and mixed up inside

And maybe I can use it all for good

It's so easy to become emotionally numb,

To be bitter towards myself and all who've hurt me in my life

I try to use my struggles for something positive

But I live my life on the brink of suicide

By wishing one-minute life

But continual thoughts of death

Wishing someone would recognize I'm hurting

By offering me patience and understanding

That can only come from one who has also endured hurt

Who has struggled and found hope beyond just medication and false love

I know that my life is abnormal

In relation to others who never knew this struggle

So, please don't pass judgment

You're only adding to open wounds

And enabling me

To have an unforgiving heart

So that when I stand before God in judgment

He will not in mercy forgive my imperfections

Because I have taken my life

From going mad inside

which to me would have been

worth it all

But I'd never hear the words

"Well done, good and faithful servant."

Then I will be tormented

In another life

While Satan laughs

Because his demons have served their purpose

Reflection: God is still in control

Scripture: "Pile your troubles on God's shoulders he'll carry your load, he'll
help you out."

Psalms 55:22 The Message

Your Thoughts

_____

_____

_____

_____

_____

Manic

My mind is gone

They say I'm crazy

Nobody's home

She's crazy

I don't act cool

I act a fool

Now I'm manic pretty

No more depression city

Now I may be tripping

Somewhat demented

but only a smidgen

I hear voices

Some of them have names

Adrenaline in my veins

Tonight my name is Jane

I'm breaking limits

I am not going to stop until I see ambulance lights

I'm going mad tonight

I'm going completely manic tonight

Ma ma manic

Ma ma manic tonight

Reflection: When your actions are different from your stated values, you live in inner conflict. Deal with the internal conflict so that what's inside you will be reflected on the outside.

Scripture: "Keep a cool head. Stay alert. The Devil is poised to pounce, and would like nothing better than to catch you napping. Keep your guard up. You're not the only ones plunged into these hard times."

1 Peter 5:8-9 The Message

Your Thoughts

_____

_____

_____

_____

_____

Tormented Soul

I feel like a dildo

held tight

And played with

I have no emotions

Can anyone hear me

or is this just a dream

I'm regularly used

and tossed to the side

Just a body vacant of a soul

feels like I'm losing my mind

And my heart's yelling screams

I'm ripping to pieces

Always feeling the need for approval

disappointed and scared

My soul forever connected

to one too many lovers who are one-night stands

My mind is like a tornado

slowing enough to gain more speed

My heart is hardened

from my hatred of men

I will never be the same

I'm worn to shreds

Pieces of me lost

gone forever

How can I make this madness end

before suicide makes it too late

Haunting memories attacking me

forcing me to go completely insane

I just want a life that makes sense

instead of still being a little girl in the corn fields

Used and abused by my uncle

merely tossed to the side

I feel I was damned from the beginning of my life

I never knew what it was like to be truly loved

And now my sick and demented perception

is what's holding me back from feeling positive emotions

I feel worthless a little useless

like a dildo

Just some man's easy score

that's all I feel I'll ever be

No one understands

how gloomy my world is

My worst nightmares are unreal

my dreams have always been crushed

I've slitten my wrist

and watched the blood rush out

Giving up on my life

I no longer want to fight

No matter how I try to forgive

my mind and body are shaking in fear

I'm just a dildo

just a scared little girl

My innocence was stolen

wishing the memories were forgotten

Over twenty years later it's still haunting me

running the opposite way from all my fears in life

Reflection: Turn you obstacles into opportunities. Your past shouldn't dictate your future. If you have flashbacks, don't turn around and give up so easily. Figure out how to work through them so that you can heal.

Scripture: " Whatever I have, wherever I am, I can make it through anything in the one who makes me who I am."

Philippians 4:13 The Message

Your Thoughts:

_____

_____

_____

_____

_____

Suicide

I pretend to be happy

instead of opening up about my feelings

Because it's easier for others to judge my imperfections

then it is for you to get to know me

Most people look through me

never acknowledging my true identity

You distance yourself from me

as if I'm not human at all

Why doesn't anybody ever listen

instead, you're giving advice about things you've never gone through

Oh it's easy to pass judgment on me

now I have to live with a label

Missing screws

Looney tune or crazy fool

Some even say I'm just trying to get attention

then to see that my pain is for real

I'd rather be alone

because the rejection is so overwhelming

So instead I cry when you want to talk

I'm afraid to be held or touched

So I push you away

It's easier for me to distance myself

Than believe you when you say

"I'll never hurt you"

It's hard for me to smile when I'm hurting

Even harder for me when I want to talk, and you won't understand

This is why I'd rather die

then deal with any more rejection in life

Reflection; Don't let people or situations get you to the point of giving up on life.

Scripture: " I call Heaven and Earth to witness against you today: I place before you Life and Death, Blessing and Curse. Choose life so that you and your children will live. And love God, your God, listening obediently to him, firmly embracing him. Oh yes, he is life itself, a long life settled on the soil that God, your God, promised to give your ancestors, Abraham, Isaac, and Jacob."

Deuteronomy 30: 19-20 The Message

Your Thoughts

Must I Endure

Must I Endure

so much horrifying pain

The voices nobody else hears

the people nobody else sees

Why does it happen to me

over and over again

Am I being punished

for all the bad I've done

Maybe I should've listened to my parents more

paid more attention to children's church

Why am I singled out

I just don't understand

And I know I shouldn't question God

but why me, Lord

Is there something extraordinary

in my life you want me to do

Or must I continue to endure

this horrifying pain

Reflection: Instead of praying for an easier life pray to be a stronger person

Scripture; " God's a safe house for the battered, a sanctuary during bad times. The moment you arrive, you relax; you're never sorry you knocked."

Pslams 9:9-10 The Message

Your Thought

_____

_____

_____

_____

_____

Mangled Wings

My mind has churned to its lowest low

mangled wings

Broken dreams

misery please, just set me free

All this commotion in my head

distorted visions that I misconstrue

Along the way they've trip me up

I've plunged endlessly and can't get up

I'm in absolute desolation

I have nothing left

I'm hollow, the old me I no longer see

am I that far out of reach

Mother said it would be alright

just keep up the fight

So I keep on my game face

I'm not insubstantial, besieged or want to die

I wear it well, don't

for I am a great pretender

Underneath my smile is a tormented soul

Somebody save me, heal my mangled wings.

Reflection: Changing your thought pattern can change your life. When in me start believing that God can turn every negative into a positive, you're on the right track for a triumphant life.

Scripture: "I've told you all this so that trusting in me, you will be unshakable and assured, deeply at peace. In this godless world you will continue to experience difficulties. But take heart! I've conquered the world."

John 16:33 The Message

Your Thoughts

_____

_____

_____

_____

_____

Magic Pill

I feel there is too much on my mind

too much time to think

Too much time of reliving past hurts

wishing there was a magic pill to make things different

In this moment I want to be alone

staring at these four walls

With my past demons holding me down

to remember past hurts

Wishing there was a magic pill to make things different

in my mind I'm on the brink of insanity

I'll use busy work for a distraction

and seek meaningless friendship from others

They'll lie and say they understand

tonight I'll cry a river

When I'm in a state of depression and reliving past hurts

I wish there was a magic pill to make life different

Reflection: Do not tie your life to people and material things because this will lead to disappointment and bitterness. Instead link your life to an aspiration to have a happy life.

Scripture: "Trapped by a seige, I panicked. "Out of sight, out of mind," I said. But you heard me say it, you heard and listened. Be brave. Be strong. Don't give up. Expect God to get here soon.

Psalms 31:22,24 The Message

Your Thoughts

_____

_____

_____

_____

_____

Prayer

Dear God, I realize that I may be faced with some form of depression and anxiety in my life. Therefore, I pray for your peace that surpasses all my understanding. However, I also pray for the right spirit, that I not be stuck in my negative thinking, but open to You helping me change my thought pattern. This I pray in Jesus name. Amen

Abuse, Sharper Than a Two-Edged Sword

"Abuse from a male or female in any form is abuse and will not disappear on account
of you thinking they will change."

Abusive Union

This unification is getting bleak

I don't think I've found the love I seek

My future is seemingly black

to the past I wish I could go back

The relationship's success

is becoming less and less

I have poured out my soul and heart

but we remain miles apart

I have exposed the real me

you still abuse me

I will not forget

but you will regret

All I had to offer was me

you destroyed what others used to see

My heart, love, and desire

yielded me your angry fire

Feeling less amused

but totally confused
I have lost who I used to be

so I hide deep within me

My hate for you is so deep

it even robs me of sleep

I have so much emotional pain

like when you put the knife deep in my veins

No, it's not my fault you always cheat

it's your desire I do not meet

To myself I must confess

not to get others involved in my mess

In the world, you can only help a few

I only wanted to give you a life that was true

There's a lot more to him than meets the eye

he was an abuser and loved to lie

His deceit had no bounds

he needed to hear my terrified screams

Now I see my bumps, bruises, and I'm stressed

I've tried to cover it up my best

My love for him, I do not deny

so many times I wanted to curl up and die

I couldn't push an anymore

so I closed the door

Hide obscurity

lost all purity

my last desire from this mess

Is that I find love and total success

I should have known depending on a male

I was destined for hell

I know the seclusion is a must

so that I can learn to love and trust

I must depend on God

I hope to find true love in the end

I must have been insane

to let me go, never letting my inner beauty show

Time to allow me to heal

forever staying true to who I am

Reflection: God, give me strength. God will always give you enough power
when you're ready to take that next step.

Scripture: "Don't you know anything? Haven't you been listening? God doesn't
come and go. God last. He's creator of all you can see or imagine He doesn't get
tired out, doesn't pause to catch his breath. And he knows everything, inside
and out. He energizes those who get tired"

Isaiah 40:28-31 The Message

Your Thoughts

Escaping Alcatraz

Fascinated by his charisma

you captivated my heart and soul

With a promised of undying love

you place upon my hand a ring

Reputation is all that matters in your eyes

a trophy piece in front of the guys

Declaring me to be your Queen

pledging always to be my King

The ring placed upon my hand

became a symbol of torture and trepidation

With a guarantee of more to come

your fortress my Alcatraz

Glowing turned to dimness

depression would be a frequent visitor

Your once hypnotic attraction turned to a constant fury

my heart and soul now a prisoner guarded by the warden

Breaking out to escape from my sorrow

I've become implicit speaking in silent thought

Seeking liberation from my hell on earth

by ending my anguish in this life

Reflection: Rushing water flows swiftly; it's constant pressure washes away boulders. This is like an abusive relationship. You win the battle against abuse by overwhelming your abuser.

Scripture: "There is no room in love for fear. Well-formed love banishes fear. Since fear is crippling, a fearful life- fear of death, fear of judgment is one not fully formed in love." 1 John 4;18 The Message

Your Thoughts

_____

_____

_____

_____

_____

Dear God

Dear God,

Help me out of the horrific sad, tale of years of abuse

I gave him all my heart

Yet he beat it into a million pieces

He was a great pretender

Manipulated my heart

His words were loving

His eyes were tender

And his hands always gentle

But that was in the beginning

Now there are only cuss words

Now swinging hands

Now rage-filled eyes

His words are brutal

His eyes look as if he's deranged

His hand violent

And his heart malicious

Beaten around like a punching bag

Thrown against a wall one time too many

Like I was a rage doll

If I tried to leave

I was served two black eyes, and a bloody lip

My soul left this battered body

Emotionless with only the cuts and bruises

No tears left to cry

Wishing my heart would not beat

Believing I am nothing

Please help me

Sincerely,

The Battered Woman

Reflection: Why continue to make excuses for scars and bruises? You are worth more than being someone's doormat or punching bag.

Scripture: "Husbands, go all out in love for your wives. Don't take advantage of them"

Colossians 3:19 The Message

Your Thoughts

Will He Cry

If he kills me tonight,

will he cry

Knuckle headed friends thrown at me left and right,

while his love has once again turned to rage.

Telling me my best isn't good enough

what more can I give

Go ahead you think you're a man now

throwing me from the wall to the floor

So if he kills me tonight

will he cry

All my strength is drained,

with no more life left in me

I'm drowning in my blood,

time stood still

My voice is silenced and my eyes now distant

no more fear in me

If he kills me tonight,

will he cry

Reflection: Let no one ever mistreat you leaving you with bumps and bruises. They should instead be a living reflection of God's kindness.

Scripture: "God said, "What have you done! The voice of your brother's blood is calling me from the ground."

Genesis 4:10 The Message

Your Thoughts

_____

_____

_____

_____

_____

Til Death Do Us Part

I returned from Iraq

it was a long deployment

Dealing with PTSD

I was no longer me

We had our first argument this morning

I forgot he didn't like Cheerios

He called me things that hurt to my soul

I know he's sorry, he didn't mean it

Then the most beautiful roses came with a card

That read I Love You Til Death Do Us Part

Last night, I did not answer my cell phone on the first ring but the third

When I got home, he threw me into the wall

He started choking me

I thought it was a painful dream

Not again, this isn't real

I woke to my left eye sealed shut and swollen

bruises all over my body

I know he's sorry he didn't mean it

Because a new Coach purse lay on the bed with a card

That read I Love You Til Death Do Us Part

Last night he beat me yet again

and it was like thunder rolling

If I leave how will I survive

How will I get money

I'm terrified of him and even more afraid to leave

I know he's really sorry this time

He didn't mean it

he's going to change

Because I got a new ten karat diamond ring and a card

That read I Love You Til Death Do Us Part

Last night, he beat me

It was the worst of all

I never saw such rage in his eyes

I felt like a prisoner of war

46

And then the casket came

with the most exotic arrangement of blood red roses and a card

That read I Love You Til Death Do Us Part

Reflection: Love should not invoke fear or pain. Gifts should be given out of love not guilt for our transgressions. Walking away is hard but you will have the strength when you are ready to take control of your destiny.

Scripture: "I waited and waited and waited for God. At last he looked; finally he listened. He lifted me out of the ditch, pulled me from deep mud. He stood me up on a solid rock to make sure I wouldn't slip

Psalms 40:1-2 The Message

Prayer

Our Heavenly Father, as I turn to You in faith and give my burdens to You, I ask that you would supply me with the strength I need to get out of an abusive relationship. Help me to turn to you during my time of need, and in doing so I will find hope and peace. Remove the scales from my eyes, and make me see the reality of what's really in front of me. Thank you for protecting me and keeping me as I serve you. This I pray in Jesus name. . Amen.

Relationships

"The ocean is our time spent together, and the journey is the relationship, but trust is the anchor that helps us survive the many storms at sea."

Unnecessary Absurdity

Love streams through our mysterious being

its daily course seems devoid of trust

Like soldiers marching out of cadence

the jaded soul trembles in total disarray

Why do we keep seeing cross currents

arguments erupting into unnecessary torrents

Grasping for some form of stability in this whirlwind

the heart struggles to find some underlying issue that the mind missed

Can there still be love within so much heartbreak

that gives ways to the apparent absurdity

Our thoughts try to rationalize our behavior

our daily action cannot hide our real intentions

Reflection: Commitment is a line we must all cross. It's the difference between harmony and dysfunction. A personal commitment is our pride. It's what separate synchronization and unnecessary absurdity.

Scripture: "You never know wife: The way you handle this might bring your husband not only back to you but to God. You never know husband: the way you handle this might bring your wife not only back to you but to God."
1 Corinthians 7:16 The Message

Your Thought

Can You Look At Yourself

Can you look at yourself in the mirror

the very moment I laid eyes on you

I saw the hateration in your eyes

but I'm prepared with my Hater Raid

I did my share

in my lonely day

Hiding behind the make-up

and the Gucci shades

You can hate on my hair

my nails and my clothes

Call me a slut, or a whore

but you can never break me down to my soul

When I look at myself in the mirror

I'm confident, and don't have to feel ashamed

The reflection couldn't be any more lucid

there's never a doubt about who I am

When you look at yourself in the mirror

do you recognize what you see

Or are you just a glimmer

can you look at yourself in the mirror

Reflection: It is better to anger others by doing what you know is right, than to momentarily please them by doing what you know is wrong. Why compromise your preservation of self-respect?

Scripture: "You are one happy man when you do what's right, and one happy woman when you form the habit of justice."

Psalms 106:3 The Message

Your Thoughts

Why Lie

You tell one lie

you have to tell another one

You can try and cover them up

but the truth you can't hide

So what's the point in telling a lie

Feelings come and go

even without a storm the wind will blow

There are so few people in this world to trust in

trying to seduce naive victims with lies which don't realize

What's being called love is only lust

You speak sweet nothings in the innocents ear

but you were never sincere

Untruth can tarnish the unpolluted inside

you play them like fools because you play by your rules

You don't even think twice before you start to lie

You tell one lie

you have to tell another one

You can try to cover them up
but the truth you can't hide

So what's the point in telling a lie

Reflection: Your inner character is reflected outwardly by your honesty.
Honesty helps you keep a clear conscious.

Scripture: "If you're honest in small things, you'll be honest in big things; If
you're a crook in small things, you'll be a crook in big things.

Luke 16:10 The Message

Your Thoughts

_____

_____

_____

_____

_____

Runaway Love

How can you forgive me

when so many times I've strayed

How can you still love me

When I've caused you so much pain

Turning my back on you

in your eyes I see the hurt

Another I still desire

fulfilling my sexual thirst

You told me you loved

and would give me time and space

You tell me, please come back now

but another has taken your place

Telling you I'm not what you need

you tell me I'm dead wrong

But I feel I've been dishonest too long

you ask me what's going on

So now I'm packing, leaving you

you are standing, begging for me
I can't no longer live this lie

I can't continually hurt you anymore

I'm running away from you

and you are standing in disbelief

Why does my heart stray away

when you treat me right

Reflection: Loving enough to let go is better than being in a one-sided relationship.

Scripture: "Good sense will scout ahead for danger, Insight will keep an eye out for you. They'll keep you from making wrong turns, or following the bad directions. Wise friends will rescue you from the Temptress that smooth-talking Seductress who's" faithless to the husband she married years ago, never gave a second thought to her promises before God.

Proverbs 2:12, 16-17 The Message

Your Thoughts

_____

_____

_____

_____

_____

4th of July Celebration 5th of July Depression

It is the 4th, the 4th of July

everyone is celebrating the joining of the fireworks

All of the bright grandiose colors exploding together

making a kaleidoscope in the sky

My marriage is but an expired firecracker

set off by a bitter blowtorch of divorce

My hatred is thrown around

in many directions in life

My heart is the burnt wick

that sometimes shimmered a soft ray of hope

My trust is the soiled paper that rippled down

falling this way and that way, unsure where to come to rest

My self-esteem is the causality

balled up in knots like the parachute

My soul is the unscathed powder

protected from the blaze

But I
I am the singed outside paper

Crinkling away from everything

mentally damning the bitter blowtorch

Reflection: Holding on to anger is like grabbing a hot coal with the intention of throwing it at someone else; you're the one who gets burned

Scripture: "A person without self-control is like a house with its doors and windows knocked out."

Proverbs 25:28 The Message

Your Thoughts

_____

_____

_____

_____

_____

Friendship

A best friend is not something that just happens
a true friendship must be shaped
In friendship, the little things are what mean the most
it's remembering to say you're loved and appreciated

It's saying I'm sorry when you've made each other angry
it's not taking each other for granted
The friendship should not end over petty drama
it should continue through the years

It's respecting each others values
and supporting each other when things are going crazy
It's doing things for each other in a spirit of happiness
not out of obligation

It is not expecting perfection from each other
and allowing them to be themselves faults and all
It is creating a relationship in which the sovereignty is equal
you are best friends because

Reliance is mutual, and the commitment is reciprocal

your bond is inclusive it has no ending
You share one soul and one heart

best friends even when miles apart

Reflection: You don't choose friends,you invite them to be a part of your life. Although, some friends can be fired for bad behavior.

Scripture: "This is the very best way to love. Put your life on the line for your friends."

John 15:13 The Message

_____

_____

_____

_____

_____

Catch 22

I am totally confused

what am I to do

He only loves me

I'm in love with him

What am I going to do

Can't get you off of my mind

I don't want anyone new

But I think some time away from you will do

I still can't seem to let you go

I'm scared stiff to be with this man, and I love him so

I'm caught in a catch 22

I have no inkling what to do

Whichever way I turn I might lose

if I tell him, I'm in love

It might cause friction between us if I don't my heart still suffers

I am so confused

this situation is killing me

Ripping me in two

you're my best friend

What am I going to do

The words will roll off my lips

like a sweet love song

Reflection: Let's not look back with "what ifs" or forward in fear, but around in confidence.

Scripture: "Look at it this way. If someone has a hundred sheep and one of them wanders off, doesn't he leave the ninety-nine and go after the one? And if he finds it, doesn't he make far more over the ninety-nine who stay put?"

Matthew 18:12-13 The Message

Your Thoughts

Until You Come Home

Until you come home

nights will be colder

Days a little shorter

my heart beats A

little less swiftly

Until you come home

I know our house will feel empty

My mind aches from the constant thoughts of you

Minutes will be like hours and hours like months

While months will seem to be an eternity

Until you come home

the stars in the sky

Won't effect me

with their gleaming sparkles of light

Until I'm gazing at them in your arms

Nothing will be fulfilling

until I share it with you

Until you come home

I will not feel whole

my world is incomplete

Until that precious day

when our eyes connect

And our bodies and souls collide

in a whirlwind of bliss

When you come home

The words will roll off my lips

like a sweet song

Hello, my love

I couldn't wait for you to come home

Reflection: As a couple you are obligated to remain faithful in light of how physically far apart you are.

Scripture: "Be like house servants waiting for their master to come back from his honeymoon, awake and ready to open the door when he arrives and knocks."

Luke 12:36 The Message

Your Thoughts

_____

_____

_____

_____

_____

Prayer

Dear God, help me to be in the dark, who I pretend to be in the light. Help me always to be patient and compromising so that I may have harmony in my relationships with others. Let me always strive to improve myself so that I might more deeply love and give love. Most importantly let me have a deeper understanding of You and your will and purpose for my life. This I pray in Jesus name. Amen

True Love

.

"To experience true love is like getting a sneak preview of what heaven is like, its luminous streets of gold and the unconditional warmth of God's love."

A Mother's Love

Mother, I see

the reality of what you've done

All the sacrifices you've made for me

to make me a woman

So many times you made it clear

that I would be something

So glad that you're here

when I need you the most

You always take time to understand me

sharing your big heart and life so freely

I can never say how much I love you so

never let you go

One thing's for certain

you taught me to love God

I'm appreciative so thankful

I appreciate all you've done for me

When I cry

you're always there
You wipe every teardrop falling

your love makes every pain go away

And when I cry

you know what to say

You wrap your loving arms around me

your love makes everything go away

Reflection: A child never outgrows the need for a mother's love. A mother never outgrows the need to give love.

Scripture: "A good woman is hard to find, and worth far more than diamond."

Proverbs 31:10 The Message

Your Thoughts

_____

_____

_____

_____

True Love

I am your ring of fire, and you are my ocean

where volcanoes circle the Pacific

Building our foundation mixing into my waters

constantly sparkling with your sun rays

Always bright and blue when I am scorching

the rush of your waves cools me

Who can cool me but you

who else dares to find the bottom of my ocean

You bravely wash on my lava bed

peacefully, calmly, the gentlest sea

The wind is our voices

that speaks for the ring of fire and the ocean

Sometimes whispering

while other times singing a melody

Only the hearts

can hear

Reflection: A life without true love is a lethargic, nomadic craze. We should not put limits on love but bask in the exquisiteness of its passion

Scripture: "Love never dies. Inspired speech will be over some day some day; praying in tongues will end; understanding will reach its limit. We know only a portion of the truth, and what we say about God is always incomplete. But when the complete arrives our complete will be canceled.

1 Corinthians 13:8-10 The Message

Your Thoughts

_____

_____

_____

_____

_____

Elation

My heart is throbbing with elation

a feeling of gratification I cannot explain

I feel seduced, by you, all alone

I thought I could withstand you;I thought I could hold on

I had a case of depression

but you are my medication

So why do others say

I'm messed up in the head

I wish you were mine

and pray you would stay

I pray to make love to you every day

visions of you flow through my mind and engulf my soul

It is you I'm missing, it is your tender touch I lack

this undeniable love fills me with a soft, gentle flow

At times like this I merely close my eyes

and picture holding you and saying I Love You So.....

Reflection: Why do we love blindly and with our heart closed. Open your heart, love could be placed right beside you.

Scripture: "The person who refuses to love doesn't know the first thing about God, because God is love- so you can't know him if you don't know him." 1

John 4:7-8 The Message

Your Thoughts

_____

_____

_____

_____

_____

Glimpse of Heaven

I don't require lot of possessions

I can get by with zilch

Of all the blessings, life handed me

I've made out big on one thing

when it comes to loving you

You're my raison d'être

loving you, is like getting a glimpse of heaven

You're my only genuineness

I need you like water falls to the sea

I need you like God's mercy saves you and me

you're the optimism that stirs me

To try and try again

you're my life saver when I've fallen overboard

It's astonishing

the way you are

I can't turn back no

I've fallen in love too hard

Reflection: "True Love!!!" Trust and communication are the keys to healthy relationship. With it you fall deeper ad deeper in love.

Scripture: "How beautiful your love dear, dear friend- far more pleasing than a fine, rare wine, your fragrance more exotic than select spices. The kiss of your lips are honey, my love, every syllable you speak a delicacy to savor, Your clothes smell like the wild outdoors, the ozone scent of high mountains. Dear lover and friend, you're a secret garden, a private and pure fountain. Body and soul, you are paradise, a whole orchard of succulent fruits. Ripe apricots and pears; Nut trees and cinnamon, and all scented woods; mint and lavender, and all herbs aromatic; a garden fountain sparkling and splashing, feed by spring waters from lebanon mountains"

Song of Songs 4:10-12 The Message

Your Thoughts

_____

_____

_____

_____

_____

Soul Mate

My soul mate

do you doubt we'll bestow

A love extraordinary

and genuinely rare

Our soul's superiority

will give us no substitute

Time stands still

when I hear the deepness of your voice

If destiny has its way

your eyes will meet mine

lost in eternity

We'll travel through time

Then, the long-awaited moment

our hands touch

Mine dainty and delicate

yours masculine and rough

No thoughts will break

or suspend our pathway

When our kindred spirits meet

we'll be left to chance

Like a forceful hurricane

fate will ordain

Our hearts will cast aside

released from misery and pain

To each other's soul

we will be led

Seduction upon us

our longing fed

Our hearts for each other only

our bodies will surrender

Acknowledging each other's warmth

to my touch your touch so tender

A passionate encounter

fulfilled long at last

We'll know from then on

if this union will just pass

The future of us will be revealed then

what might our future be

will we be lovers

will we be friends

Reflection: How do you know you found your soul mate? Fondness brings
about true love, and true love brings true happiness.

Scripture: Blessed are the chosen! Blessed the guest at home in your place! We
expect our fill of good things in your house. your heavenly manse"

Psalms 65:4 The Message

Your Thought

_____

_____

_____

_____

_____

Say "I Do"

I want to say "I do" because

deep inside me, I long to love one person, you

With all my heart, my mind

my body and soul

Because I need a real confidant

to trust with all the intimacies of me

Who won't hold them against me

who loves me when I have my mood swings

Who loves the kid in me

and who sees the extraordinary perspective in me

I love to cuddle in your arms

day and night

With you thanking God for me

with me feeling set apart to have you

Marrying you is the opportunity

to grow in love and friendship

Our marriage will not fail, people fail

I will not cross the threshold into this union

expecting you to make me whole

I promise you I will take full responsibility

For my religiousness, psychological, and bodily wholeness

God created you and me

And I take half responsibility and you the other

for this marriage

Together we make a perfect union

with my total faith and understanding

In this, the potentials are limitless

our marriage will be a forever thing

I want to marry you

not only for all those things

but because

I love you

Reflection: In a significant relationship partners show themselves as they truly are.

Scripture: "Becoming one flesh no longer two bodies but one. Because God created this union of two sexes, no one should desecrate his art by cutting them apart."

Matthew 16:6 The Message

Your Thoughts

_____

_____

_____

_____

_____

Prayer

Dear God, thank you for giving me a best friend and a soul mate. A partner who loves me like the fear you. Knowing that with God our relationship will not fail because you are the center of it. Help me to help him/her in their time of need and be sensitive to his/her emotions. Most of all may you always get the glory. This I pray in Jesus name . Amen.

Why Run From God When He Is Reaching His Hand Out To You

"In life, it is never too late to change direction; to strengthen a personal relationship and our family relationships with family and most of all our relationship with God. It's never too late to run to God!

Make a Choice

You want God's anointing

I'd say pray more

But I know that you won't

I don't comprehend what's so hard

You either want to live for Him, or you don't

one day you serve Him the next day you disappear

You're so half-hearted, hurting your soul

he doesn't react right when you call

That's when you decide to stray away

he gave his life for you

A crown of thrones, pierced side, painful stripes

yet He still rose on the third day so that we can be liberated

Maybe He should just turn and act to good like you and me

God's getting tired of it

Maybe he should turn his back on you from day to day

So make a choice

What is it that you want to do

because your soul is waiting

Yes or no mama and daddy can't serve God for you

stay or go yes or no

Reflection: Being in right standing with God far outweighs holding up our worldly image.

Scripture: "Time's up! God's kingdom is here. Change your life and believe in the Message."

Mark 1:15 The Message

Your Thought

_____

_____

_____

_____

_____

Change Me

Lord I'm in need of your deliverance

I've been wallowing in sin too long

Didn't even know how deep I'd fallen in

went to the altar asking Jesus

Please help me now

and I dropped to my knees hands raised my head I bowed

Even my nature is changing

I'm feeling the Holy Spirit Rising

Speaking new life to me

you put the joy back in my life

Where there was once black and white

your grace is a kaleidoscope of light

Before you Lord

I was dirty

Filthy with sin

Lord you cleansed me from within

You blessed me with a new beginning

now I'm free

In that moment

you put your hands in my heart Lord Jesus

Now it beats

I've got Angels surrounding me

Your blood cleansed every part of me

It washed me white as snow, and I completely surrender my heart

Reflection: Cherish your soul salvation. Never undervalue it

Scripture: "You're not "doing" anything; you're. simply calling out to God, trusting him to do it for you That's salvation. With your whole being you embrace God setting things right, and the you say it right and out loud."

Romans 10:9-10 The Message

Your Thoughts

_____

_____

_____

_____

_____

The Voice of God

He is water to me

the placid spring rain that falls in the midst of my troubles

My God proves himself to me

over and over and over again

My God is vision

even fashionable of sight

God appears to me

by imparting equally day and night

He is an assortment

and also one

My God the benevolent

our continuous sun

Wow I hear his voice

sometimes through his sons and daughter

God of creation whispers

through the atmosphere, earth and stream

So diligently I serve

God for life I do not deserve

He walks with me

on this road of salvation

He tells me to pray

for the ones who need to be loved

And those who need to be touched

my God, I worship you

When I'm at my wits end

he speaks to me

My God please not only speak to me

but also a friend

Reflection: Don't take God's goodness for granted by unconsciously tuning out his voice because you are preoccupied with complaining about unanswered prayers, instead worship him because it is already done. He has spoken to you but did you hear Him?

Scripture: "Open your mouth and taste, open your eyes and see how good God is

Psalms 34:8 The Message

Your Thoughts

_____

_____

_____

_____

_____

Sweet Communion

You provide blessings

you shine like the golden son

You shower me with a refreshing rain

you are the benevolent one

In my deepest and darkest thoughts

you are within
And in all the battles I face

you help me win

You make me long to discover you

you have melted the ice from my heart

On the cross, you have bore my pain

speak to me now in the midst of the hurricane

YAHWEH-SHALOM, give me peace

YAHWEH-SHAMMAH, be eternally close to me

Lighten my darkness like a breath of heaven

shower me with your anointing

There is nothing like being in sweet communion with you

having me time in prayer

Longing to be in your presence

knowing that I belong because I safe in your arms.

Reflection: Prayer takes us into God's presence to show us his will and purpose for our lives. It's not just for blessing our activities but rather to change us from the inside out.

Scripture: "Treat my prayer as sweet incense rising; my raised hands are my evening prayers.

Psalms 14:2 The Message

Your Thoughts

_____

_____

_____

_____

_____

Prayer

Dear God, forgive me for neglecting my spiritual nurture; give me an awareness of your directions and the courage to follow. Help me to trust in you through trials and tribulations. Forgive me for demanding that you answer my prayers as I want them to be answered. Help me to be patient and to remember that you are always in complete control. Teach me to surrender me totally to You and leave my burdens at your feet. I thank you that you always do what is best for me. This I pray in Jesus name. Amen.

Prayer

Dear God, forgive me for neglecting my spiritual nurture; give me an awareness of your directions and the courage to follow. Help me to trust in you through trials and tribulations. Forgive me for demanding that you answer my prayers as I want them to be answered. Help me to be patient and to remember that you are always in complete control. Teach me to surrender me totally to You and leave my burdens at your feet. I thank you that you always do what is best for me. This I pray in Jesus name. Amen.

Lightning Source UK Ltd.
Milton Keynes UK
UKRC02n2152100818
327020UK00001B/25